ABC's with the VEJIGANTES

Written by Liz DeJesus
Illustrated by Amber Davis

Copyright © 2022 by Liz DeJesus and Amber Davis
Second Edition Printing ©2023

Library of Congress Control Number 2021925038

Paperback ISBN 9781088277706
Hardback ISBN 9798868902079
Electronic ISBN 9798868902093

Printed in the United States of America
Cover design by Amber Davis Art

Visit Our Websites!
www.LizDejesus.com
www.AmberDavisArt.com

unexpected spark
studios
who says magic can't be real?

This book is dedicated to Kristen L. Corbett. Love you forever, my darling girl.

-Liz

This book is dedicated to Mom and Nana. You aren't here to see my dream come true, but I know you're watching down, smiling proud.

-Amber

Once a year, in the streets of Ponce, on the small island of Puerto Rico, children from all over the island gather to watch the Vejigantes Parade. Every year, many artisans make costumes for people to wear during the parade.

All of the costumes and masks have different colors and designs. Some artisans use coconut shells to make the vejigante mask. Some like to use paper maché and newspaper to make their masks.

The vejigantes are an important part of Puerto Rican history. During the Fiestas de Santiago el Apostól, the vejigantes' intention is to frighten people and compel them to go back to church for Lent. A week before Ash Wednesday, vejigantes wear long, colorful robes and brightly painted masks to cause mischief. The parade has four main characters: the vejigantes, the knights, the crazy women and the elders.

The first vejigante to walk down the street has a costume that is **blue** like the Puerto Rican sky.

Azúl

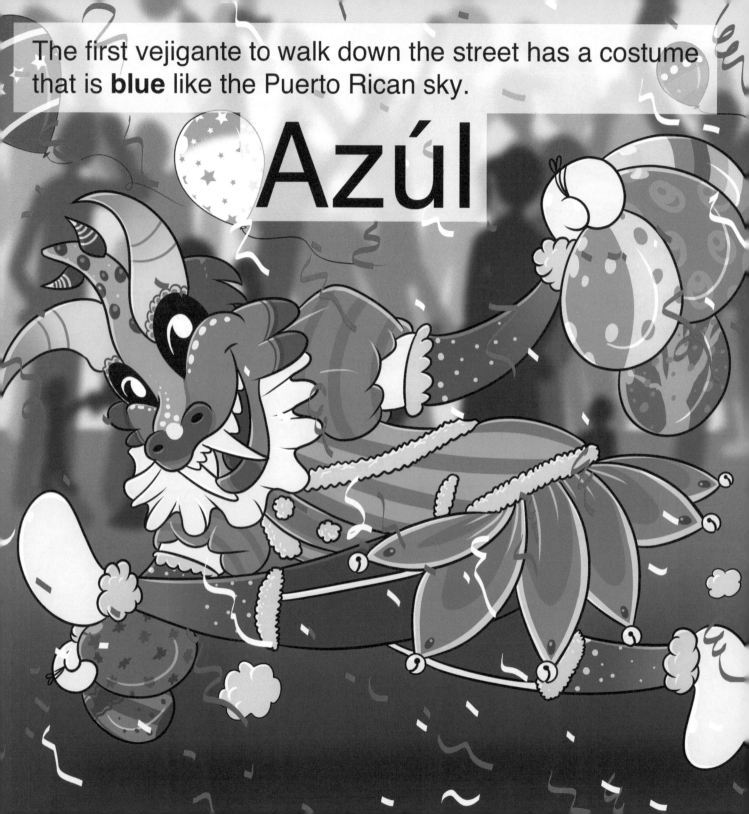

This vejigante has a mask and costume that is painted red, white, and blue like the Puerto Rican **flag**.

Bandera

The **knights** walk down the streets in their masks and costumes.

Caballeros

Chiringa

One of the vejigantes runs as he flies a **kite** past the crowd!

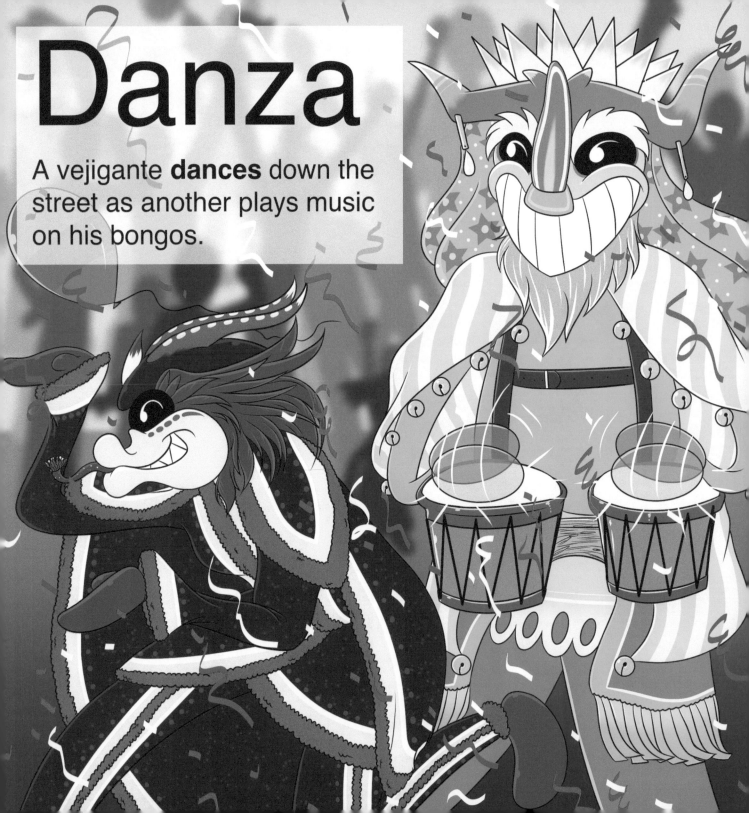

Danza

A vejigante **dances** down the street as another plays music on his bongos.

Estrellas

One of the vejigantes does cartwheels and somersaults as he displays his amazing costume and mask. It has many different size **stars** painted on it.

Flamboyán

The next vejigante costume has beautiful red **flame tree** flowers painted on his mask and costume.

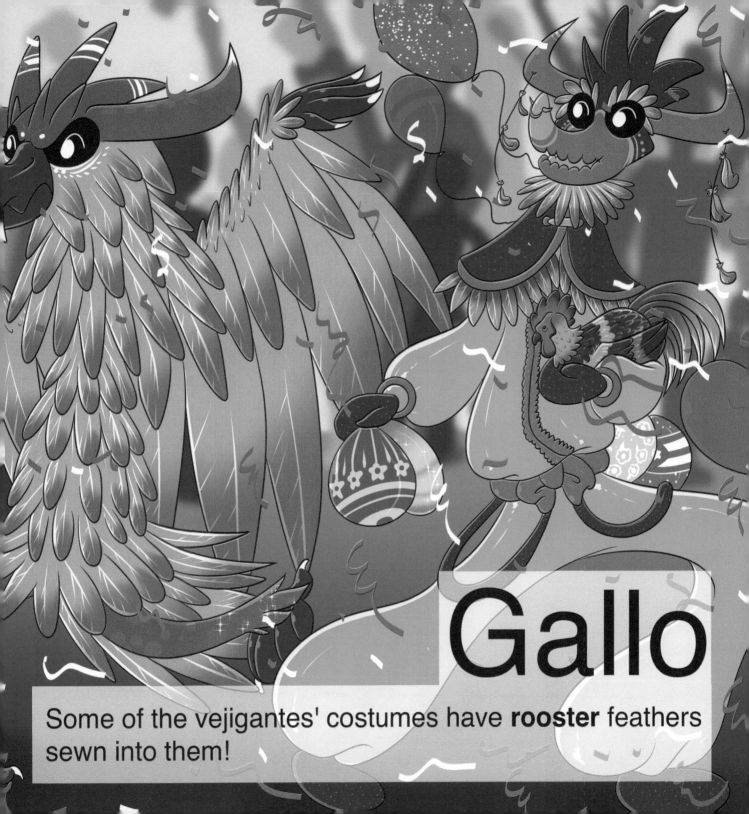

Gallo

Some of the vejigantes' costumes have **rooster** feathers sewn into them!

Hormiguero

One of the vejigantes has accidentally stepped on an **anthill**. A little girl giggles as she watches him hop on one foot trying to brush the black ants off his feet!

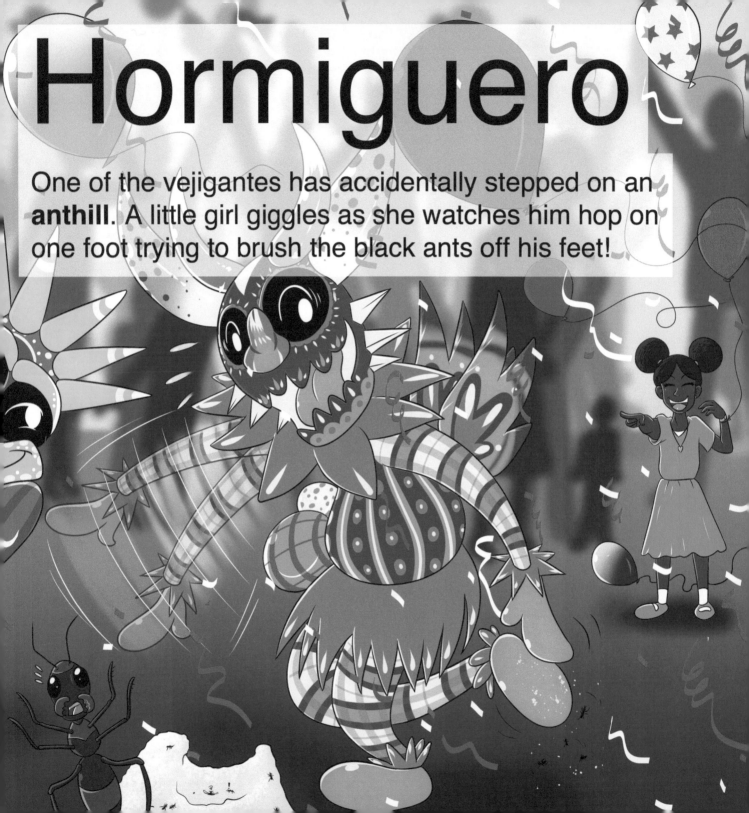

Iguana

One of the vejigantes has his pet **iguana** perched on his shoulder!

Jíbaros

Several **farmers** dance down the street as they play instruments like the guitar, cuatro, and güiro.

Kiosco

The vejigantes walk past a **kiosk** where they are selling empanadillas and alcapurrías.

Libreta

One of the vejigantes wears a costume made of reused **notebook** paper.

Lluvia

It has started to **rain** a little during the parade! Many of the vejigantes continue to dance and play.

Maracas

The elders finally make an appearance. They dance, sing, and shake their **maracas** behind the vejigantes!

Naranja

A little boy points out the vejigante that reminds him of a bright colorful **orange**.

Ñames, olivos, y plátanos

The vejigantes walk by different vendors that are lined up on the sidewalk hoping to sell their merchandise. There is a woman with a vegetable cart. She has **yams**, **olives**, and **plantains**.

The children cry in delight when they see **fifteen** vejigantes riding bikes!

Quince

Reinita

A little girl has dropped some of her piragua on the ground without realizing it!

Her father smiles and says, "Look, there is a **little queen** drinking your melted piragua by your feet!"

Sombrillas

The crazy women laugh and dance with their brightly colored **umbrellas**!

Taínos y Uvas

One of the masks is like the native **Tainos** drawing El Sol de Jayuya! And a group of knights wear purple capes. It reminds the children of **grapes**.

Verde

Several of the costumes in the parade are **green**, like the coqui that sing a nocturnal symphony night after night.

¡Coquí! ¡Coquí! ¡Coquí-quí-quí-quí! ¡Coquí!

W

W is not considered a proper Spanish letter, but appears in foreign words. In Spanish, it is called a double **ve** or double **u**. In some words, it's pronounced like **U** and in others like a **B**.

Xilófono

Another vejigante plays the **xylophone** as he dances down the street!

Yerba

One of the children points to one of the vejigantes' costumes. It has **grass** glued to the sleeves.

Zumbador

A **hummingbird** buzzes behind the vejigantes as the parade comes to an end.

The sun goes down. The parade is over. Everyone enjoyed watching the vejigantes dance and sing.

Writer: Liz DeJesus

Liz DeJesus was born and raised on the tiny island of Puerto Rico. She is the author of The Jackets, The Frost Series, Morgan, The Laurel, Girl, Mugshots, and Zombie Ever After.
Liz also is the co-founder of The Hockessin Art and Book Fair and Anime Day.

Visit her at www.LizDejesus.com

Illustrator: Amber Davis

Amber Davis is an artist born in Philadelphia, Pennsylvania who studied illustration at Moore College of Art and Design. Her love of color and humor shines brightly in her work, and she gets her inspiration from Japanese animation and manga, as well as nature. She currently resides in New Jersey with her loving, supportive husband and two children.

Visit her at www.AmberDavisArt.com

Azul = ah-sool

Bandera = bahn-deh-rah

Caballeros = kah-bah-yeh-rohs

Chiringa = Chee-reen-gah

Danza = dahn-sah

Estrellas = ehs-treh-yahs

Flamboyan = flahm-boy-ahn

Gallo = gah-yoh

Hormiguero = ohr-mee-geh-roh

Iguana = ih-gwa-nuh

Jíbaro = hee-bah-roh

Kiosko = kyohs-koh

Libreta = lee-breh-tah

Lluvia = yoo-byah

Maracas = muh-ra-kuhz

Naranja = nah-rahng-hah

ñame = nyah-meh

Olivos = oh-lee-boh

Plátano = plah-tah-noh

Quince = keen-seh

Reinita = rrey-neh-tah

Sombrilla = sohm-bree-yah

Taínos = tah-ee-noh

Uvas = oo-bah

Verde = behr-deh

Vejigante = beh-hee-gahn-teh

Xilófono = see-loh-foh-noh

Yerba = yehr-bah

Zumbador = zoom-bah-dohr

Practice your numbers with the "Quince" Vejigantes!

1 - Uno = oo-noh
2 - Dos = dohs
3 - Tres = trehs
4 - Cuatro = kwah-troh
5 - Cinco = seeng-koh
6 - Seis = seys
7 - Siete = syeh-teh
8 - Ocho = oh-choh
9 - Nueve = nweh-beh
10 - Diez = dyehs
11 - Once = ohn-seh
12 - Doce = doh-seh
13 - Trece = treh-seh
14 - Catorce = kah-tohr-seh
15 - Quince = keen-seh

Thanks for reading!

¡Gracias por leer!

Milton Keynes UK
Ingram Content Group UK Ltd.
UKHW052038090124
435708UK00003B/22